THE
ISLES OF SHOALS
THROUGH TIME

DONALD CANN, GAYLE KADLIK,
AND JOHN GALLUZZO

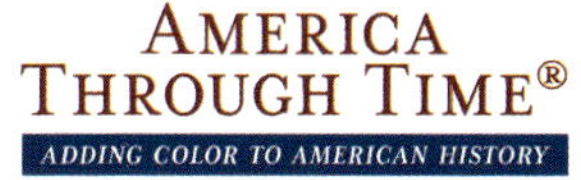

To all lovers of the Isles of Shoals, past, present and especially future.
You will come back!

America Through Time is an imprint of Fonthill Media LLC
www.through-time.com
office@through-time.com

Published by Arcadia Publishing by arrangement with Fonthill Media LLC
For all general information, please contact Arcadia Publishing:
Telephone: 843-853-2070
Fax: 843-853-0044
E-mail: sales@arcadiapublishing.com
For customer service and orders:
Toll-Free 1-888-313-2665

www.arcadiapublishing.com

First published 2020

ISBN 978-1-63500-105-1

Typeset in Mrs Eaves XL Serif Narrow
Printed and bound in England

INTRODUCTION

In a way, we are blessed.

History is propelled by incremental changes that we barely notice as time progresses. Sometimes, when major events occur, major changes follow. Storms, fires and other catastrophes tear down what man has built, forcing us to replace beloved buildings and monuments with either facsimiles or entirely new structures. Either way, something is lost: tradition, a sense of familiarity, a feeling of comfort.

Strangely, this phenomenon can work in reverse as well. When an industry dies, and a community depended on that industry, a catastrophic change occurs. Once relevant and thriving, a town stagnates. Places where captains of those industries lived and built the most spacious homes of their generation simply freeze in time; with no new money, there are no new homes. Some of America's most wonderful and architecturally interesting towns symbolize this phenomenon. Edgartown, on Massachusetts' Martha's Vineyard, is one such place. When the whaling industry died, the Federal style homes there stood still. In Cape May, New Jersey, it was the Victorian era and the end of the vacation age.

And then there are the Isles of Shoals.

The Shoals certainly had their moment. We can't think of them without evoking the poetry of Celia Thaxter or imagining Uncle Oscar Laighton rowing from Appledore to Star. We can't imagine the skyline without the Oceanic Hotel or the iconic chapel. Yes, the Shoals had their heyday, but we never said that a community freezing in time was a bad thing.

Instead, we are blessed. We are blessed by the fact that we can walk in the footsteps of Celia Thaxter on Appledore Island, and we can wander her gardens. We can understand the life that she lived on the island, the beauty of the seasonality. We can wander the natural areas of the island that gained their names more than a century ago—Siren's Cove, Devil's Dance Floor, and more—and consider what the famed artists of the day, like Childe Hassam, thought of them when they visited with Celia. We can stand on the island and hear the faded whispers of the representatives of the Japanese and Russian governments who visited during their stay in Portsmouth to seek terms for a peaceful settlement to their 1905 war, coaxed to the New Hampshire coastline by President

Theodore Roosevelt to do so. We can also see the march of history through the relics of the island's military past, a radar tower and a Life-Saving Service station.

We are blessed because we can look out to Duck Island and watch as a bald eagle flying by rouses the hundreds of waterfowl resting on the island, a phenomenon as natural today as it was 100, 500 or 1,000 years ago. Today, we see a seal colony that might not be as familiar to the Laightons in their day. We can cruise to White Island and circle the historic lighthouse that still warns mariners of the dangers of the rocky Shoals themselves. This particular structure has been doing so since 1859, and even with the global positioning system and other navigational tools and perks, boaters still gain comfort by looking up from the helm and seeing its guiding flashes. And we can check out Smuttynose, always remembering the nefarious story of the murder that occurred there once upon a time.

When we get to Star, we can tread the same pathways that thousands upon thousands of summer revelers have trodden before. We can sit on the porch of the Oceanic, perhaps in the same spot that Uncle Oscar once rocked. We can wander back to the chapel and consider how many souls have found peace in this very space. We can peruse the cottages, step through the turnstile and think about what John Smith must have seen on his arrival in 1614. Yes, the known human history on the Isles of Shoals goes back that far, and even farther. Native Americans had been there for at least 400 years prior to Smith's arrival.

There have been changes. The first Oceanic Hotel is gone, but the second one remains. Travelers from the past would recognize it, but point out minor changes here and there. The John Smith Monument on Star used to have a column, with three Turks' heads on it. The Appledore Hotel is gone, as is Celia's home. The White Island Lighthouse is the second to stand on-site. And the old steamboats that once chugged to the Shoals from Portsmouth have given way to more modern vessels.

But for every physical loss, there is spiritual continuation. Visitors to Star still laugh with giddiness each summer as they come ashore, just like their forbears did a century ago, anticipating a day, a week, a summer of enjoyment. Gulls, terns and other birds of the sea still fly about and cry their familiar cries, as they have for generations. Candle lantern processions still march to the chapel in the stillness of a New England summer night. Yachts still toss their spinnakers to the wind just offshore. And the epic and unending battle of sea versus rock, the crashing of waves on the shore, shows no sign of slowing down any time soon.

The Isles of Shoals are a throwback in time unlike many others, a place where time slows down, and where time has even stopped in places. It's a place where we can witness the grandeur of nature in its rawest emotions, and where we can walk through four, five, six centuries of human history, and still be back to the Oceanic in time for a communal dinner with friends.

The Isles of Shoals are jewels of the New England coast, accessible to all.

And in that way, we are blessed.

1

5

STAR ISLAND

BIRTH OF A DESTINATION: The Isles of Shoals transformed in the Industrial Age when the concept of the vacation arose. There were good times to be had in exclusive places—resorts, of sorts—where people could make their escape from the turmoil of expanding cities. Along the New England coast, from Bar Harbor to Block Island, steamboats ferried revelers to places of peace, of quiet, and rest. The Isles of Shoals and community of Gosport, formerly a thriving fishing village, became just such a place. (LOC)

THE FIRST OCEANIC HOUSE: The Appledore House, on nearby Appledore Island, had a competitor on Star Island when John Poor opened "The Oceanic" on Star Island. His advertisement read: "This new and elegant Hotel will open July 1st, 1873, with ample accommodation for five hundred guests. The location, scenery, climate, and facilities for boating, bathing, and fishing are unsurpassed." Weekly rates were $3.50-4.00. In 1875 this hotel burned down. The Oceanic stood where the tennis court is today. (SIC/DJC)

THE NEW OCEANIC HOUSE: The new Oceanic was hastily constructed in 1875 by building a new Mansard style building and linking it to existing buildings. This view exaggerates the length of the mansard (count the windows). It also reflects the first renovations to the hotels. The space between the Gosport Hotel and the main section was originally open and the porch wrapped around it. Note the differences in the postcard image, including the railing, stairways, landscaping, and the bump out on the Oceanic. (SIC/SIC)

THE ATLANTIC HOUSE: Pioneer Shoals resident Lemuel B. Caswell owned the Atlantic House. After a fire in 1866 it was rebuilt in 1869. It anchored the south end of the new Oceanic Hotel. The old photo shows the first floor at ground level. When it was made part of the Oceanic it was boosted up. The main freshwater cistern is under the Atlantic House. Note the addition of a dormer and the enclosed fire escape. (SIC/PA)

BOATS AT THE PIER: Since the 1870s, change has taken place at Star Island, but much has stayed the same. From the old to the new picture you can see that chimneys have disappeared. Fire escapes have been added and enclosed. The shed on the pier also disappeared. The buildings in the foreground are the Founders motel unit, the Rutledge Marine Laboratory, and Brookfield Center. The boats at the pier are somewhat similar. (SIC/DJC)

 When the original Caswell house burned in 1866, Caswell bought the Berry House (left), built the Gosport House and incorporated both stretches into his hotel. Note Cottage A to the left, as well as the number of stories in the two hotel buildings. (PHS/DJC)

 The Gosport House became part of the new Oceanic Hotel. At first both structures were not attached, other than by the porch. It was not long before the Gosport Hotel was built up a story and the area was filled in with a one-story addition, accommodating Elliot Hall and a dining room. Note the dormer on the Berry house. (DJC)

THE PORCH: There has not been a lot of change to the Oceanic porch from the old photo to the new one. The porch is still the main gathering place on the island, still the place to sit in a rocking chair and just look at the water and rocks. This photo shows that the second set of stairs are gone, as well as the bump-out window on the third floor and the gaslights. (SIC/DJC)

THE PINK PARLOR: Of all the rooms off the lobby, the Pink Parlor retains the ambiance of the nineteenth century. The wallpaper, Victorian furniture and the wall decorations all bring us back to a time when things on the island were more formal. (SIC/SIC)

A Lively Place: The Pink Parlor is far from a museum room as many activities are held here. This is a photo of a performance of a Victorian play during a Historical Society of the Isles of Shoals conference. (SIC/DJC)

THE DINING ROOM: The dining room was built in what was open space between the Gosport Hotel and new Oceanic Hotel. The old exterior windows are visible. The modern photo shows part of the wall of the Oceanic side removed. On the same side you can see part of the exterior door that still leads to the lobby. Note the chairs in each photo appear to be original to the hotel period, but are different. (SIC/DJC)

THE LOBBY: The Oceanic lobby is the information, retail and meeting center of the island. There are fewer decorations and features in the old photo than in the new. The doors to the right of the desk originally led outside, but now lead to the dining room. (SIC/DJC)

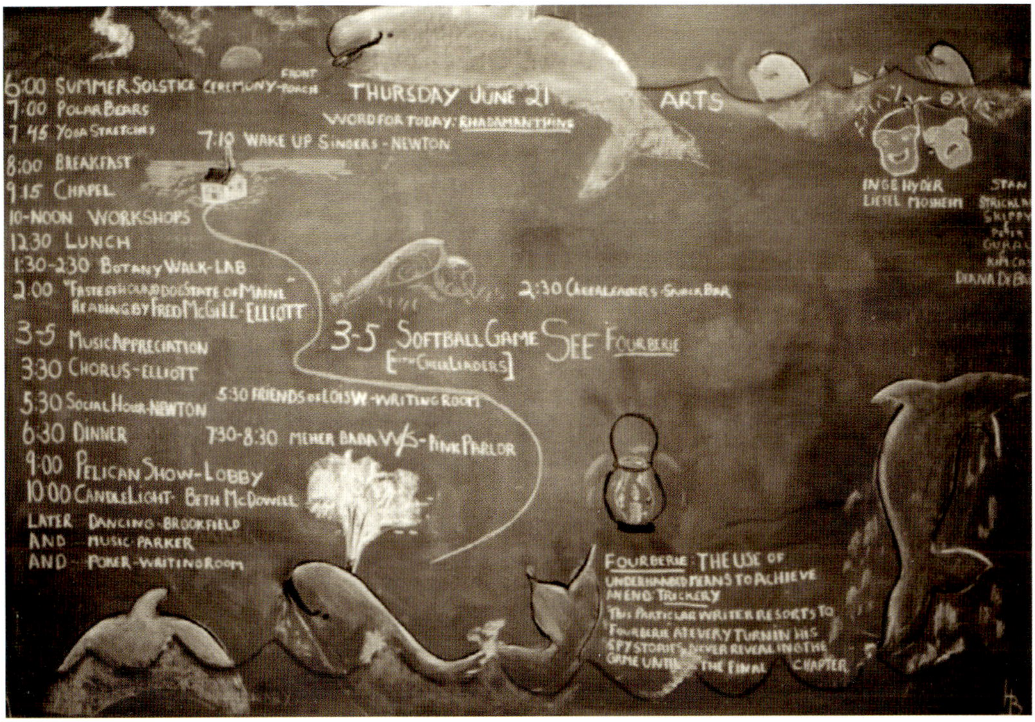

THE LOBBY BLACKBOARD: When the first blackboard was put in the lobby is unknown, but no one can remember not reading it at least twice daily to work out a personal schedule for the day. Even in the days of cell phones reading the schedule on the blackboard(s) in the lobby is as much a tradition as any another tradition on Star. (SIC/DJC)

THE BOOK STORE: Meeting, reading or just relaxing in front of the bookstore continues as long as there are tables and chairs in the lobby. At first what is now a window for the bookstore was the store's counter, and at that store, many things other than books, such as daily needs, were sold. (SIC/DJC)

THE SNACK BAR: The snack bar is always a good place to hang out in the evening. Ice cream, lime rickeys, milkshakes or coffee and tea were all favorites after dinner or before and after chapel. Games were and still are played late into the night. The ladies with the pitchers are taking water to their rooms. Treats, games and hot water are still the things that make the snack bar a favorite place, always tended by YFSBP =Your Friendly Snack Bar Pelican. (SIC/DJC)

THE GIFT SHOP: The Star Island Gift Shop was established in 1968 by volunteers Edith Doolittle and Ruth Coe. It operates as a committee of the Isles of Shoals Association (ISA). The Star Island Corporation originally operated the bookstore and the lobby store. Now all the stores are operated by the Isles of Shoals Association, which was founded in 1896 in order to organize conferences on Star Island. All profits support ISA programs and the Star Island Corporation. (SIC/DJC)

THE PEL SHOW: The Pelicans are the staff that are needed to open, run and close Star Island each year. Most Pelicans are in their late teens and early twenties and work hard. They have their own traditions, one of which is the "Pel Show." Each week the show is put on in the hotel lobby for the conferees, always a treat for young and old. (SIC/DJC)

THE POWER HOUSE: Built in 1960, the power house provides electoral power to Star Island by means of diesel engines. In 1873, the lights in the Oceanic were lit by gas and the gas plant was at the location of the building now known as the Shack, which we can see in the background. The first diesel engine to produce electric power was installed in the building known as the Art Barn. Today the diesel engines are supplemental to electricity produced by 420 solar panels installed on the island. (SIC/DJC)

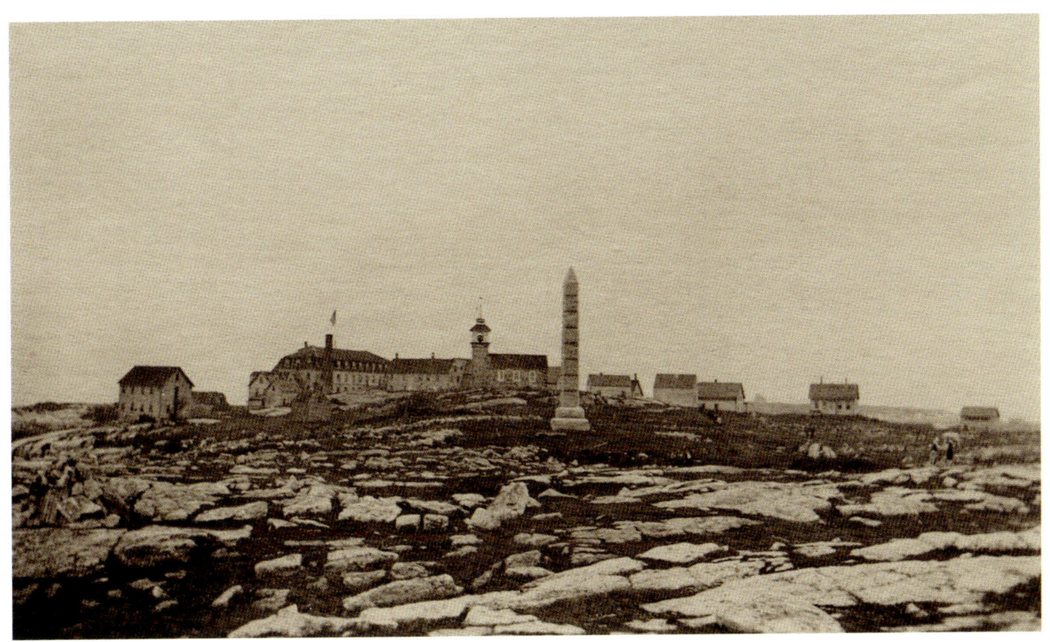

PROGRESS: Except for the 420 solar panels and the growth of the vegetation, much is the same in the new view. There are some structural changes in the buildings. The gable end of Vaughn Cottage with its two windows, between the chapel and Tuck Monument, is easy to see, but others are hidden by the vegetation. (SIC/DJC)

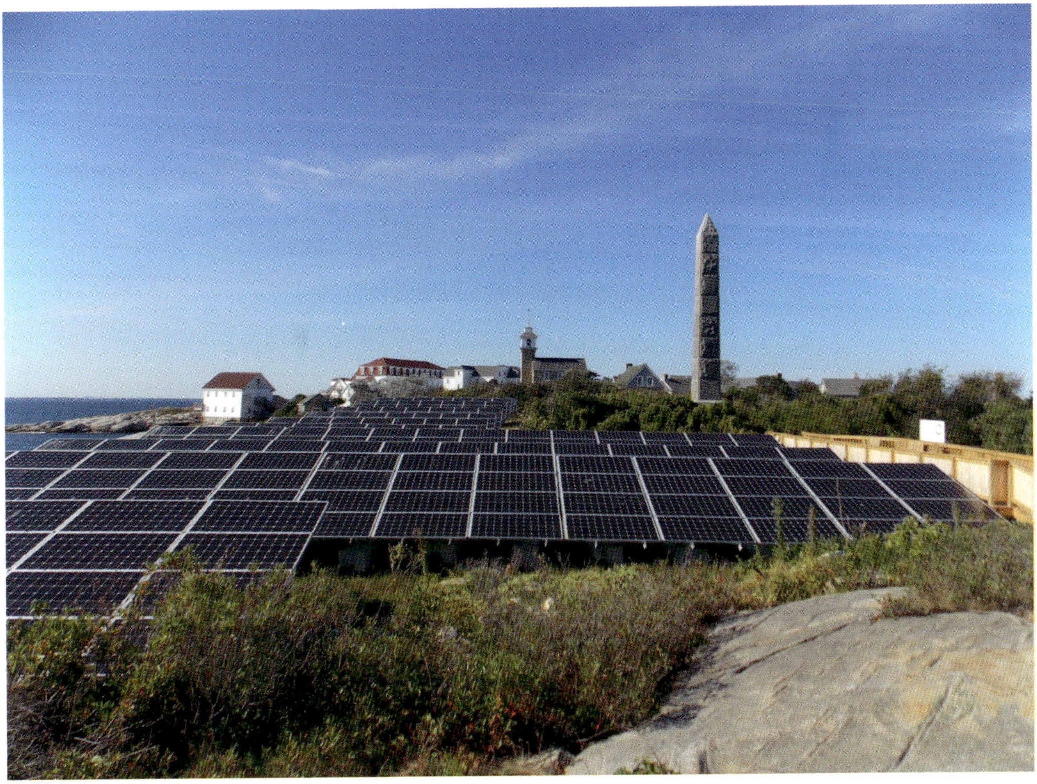

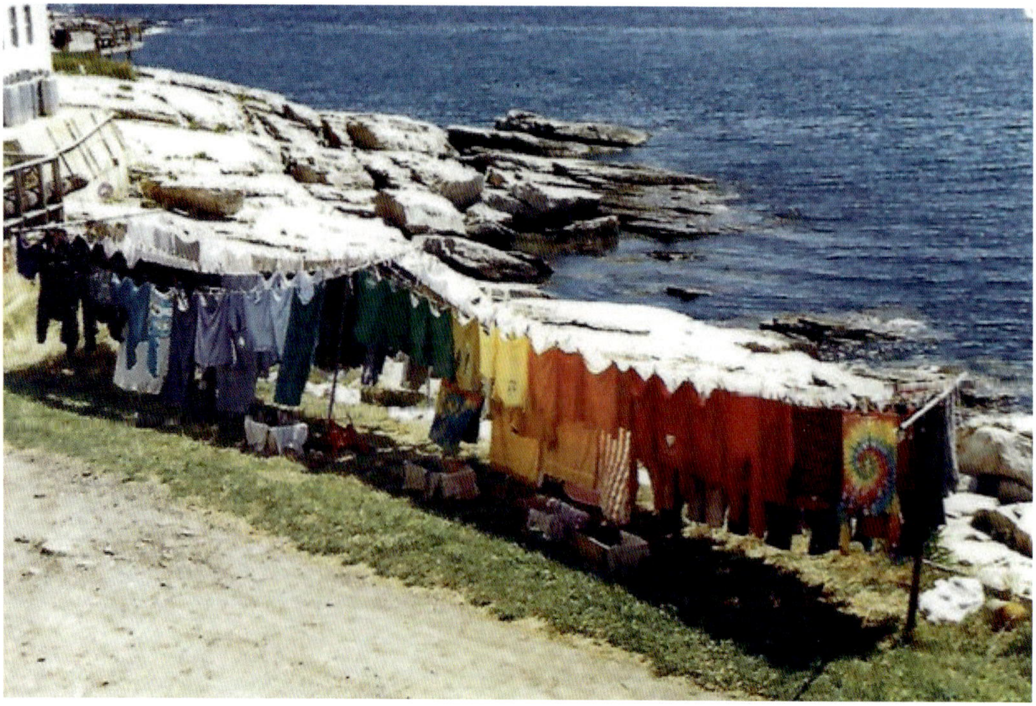

THE CLOTHESLINE: The operation of a conference center produces lots of laundry. How much of the laundry that is washed on island or sent off island to be washed changes from time to time. When the laundress is also an artist, the clothesline reflects it with a colorful arrangement, a tradition established by Meg Scheone, laundress from 1990 to 2002. The new photo was taken at the end of the season when there are fewer guests and staff. (SIC/DJC)

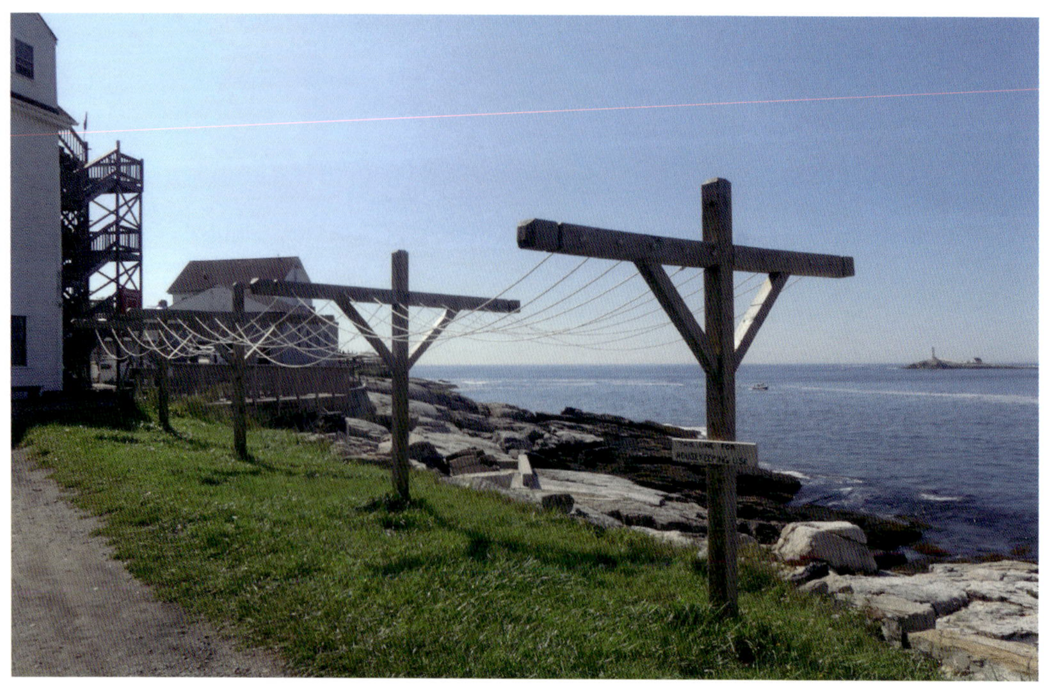

SHACK: In this view of Shack, note the old truck in the foreground of the older image—undoubtedly a vehicle well utilized for transporting island needs such as food, luggage and materials to and from the pier. To the left of Shack now stands the Paint Shop where Pelicans work on projects resulting in island improvement. Nichols, visible in the foreground, is a music studio. Island staff can often be found here practicing for the much-anticipated weekly entertainment known as Pel Show. (SIC/DJC)

CONFERENCE NOTICES: Each year the Star Island Cooperation publishes "The Blue Book," which lists all the conferences for the upcoming season. Each individual conference also sends notices to people who regularly attend and those who may be interested in going to that conference. The first notice is at the beginning of the conference period, the second is of another time, looking back at some of the history of the Shoals. (SIC/ISHRA)

CONFERENCE PHOTO: A group photo of each conference group, as well as staff, is a very old tradition on Star Island. Conferees each summer will go to Vaughn Cottage to find a group photo of their grandparents, the year they were Pelicans at Star, or attended a conference. The new photo is a reunion of Pelicans and the families that attended a conference on a Labor Day weekend. (SIC/DJC)

THE READING ROOM: Vaughn Cottage's interior is well finished and appointed. The reading room, on the right side as you come in the front door, is a favorite place. There is a library of books related to the sea and books on the history of the Isles of Shoals. Much of the original features are still in place from the time the cottage was built in 1960. The Vaughn curator is available during the summer season for information and tours. (SIC/DJC)

THE BEACH: Uncle Oscar with his boat the *Wild Duck* are at the beach. You can see the shelter at the end of the pier and rowboats for use of the hotel guests at the float. In the second image one swimmer looks like she is coming in, while others are still in the water and some are trying to make up their minds. There are still boats at the float that can be taken out by conferees. (PA/DJC)

GOING TO THE BOAT: In the early view people are headed to the boat. Notice the well, gaslight and the landscaping. In the second view, also taken from the front of the Oceanic, it looks like people are coming off and going on the boat. The gardens have been replaced with grass and the pump has a shelter built over it, now called the Wellhouse. The shelter on the pier as well as the gaslight are gone. (LOC/DJC)

ON THE FRONT LAWN: As long as there have been conferences, there have been activities on the lawn in front of the Oceanic, from formal, as in the circle with Uncle Oscar in a chair in the middle, to very informal. At the end of a season, when it gets dark relatively early, with a laptop and a big white truck, conferees can have a movie on the front lawn. (SIC/DJC)

THE ART BARN: The Art Barn building once served as an icehouse. It was the location for the first generator of electrical power. In 1960 the electrical generator was moved to the new utility building. At that point this building was repurposed to be used for art activities. (SIC)

THE POND: Because of the thick overgrowth the present-day photo of the pond had to be taken as a separate photo. (DJC/DJC)

THE SUMMER HOUSE: The simple structure on Star Island that has gained icon status is the Summer House. It was built on the site of the colonial Fort Star in the hotel period. No one knows how many times it has been rebuilt. The Summer House is a favorite place for day-trippers to have a picnic. It is also a favorite place for all to watch the sun go down. (SIC/DJC)

2

SIGHTS OLD SHOALERS KNOW WELL

Around the Isles of Shoals, and even ashore, landmarks capture the history of the people who have visited, lived, worked and played on the islands. They come in many forms, from natural settings that captured the imaginations of Victorian-era artists to buildings that have withstood the ravages of time, to monuments erected in bygone eras to memorialize parts of the greater tale. Here, then, are reminders of years gone by on the Isles of Shoals, like the sundial at the eastern end of the Oceanic Hotel on Star, the triangular stone base of which was originally part of the John Smith Monument. (DJC)

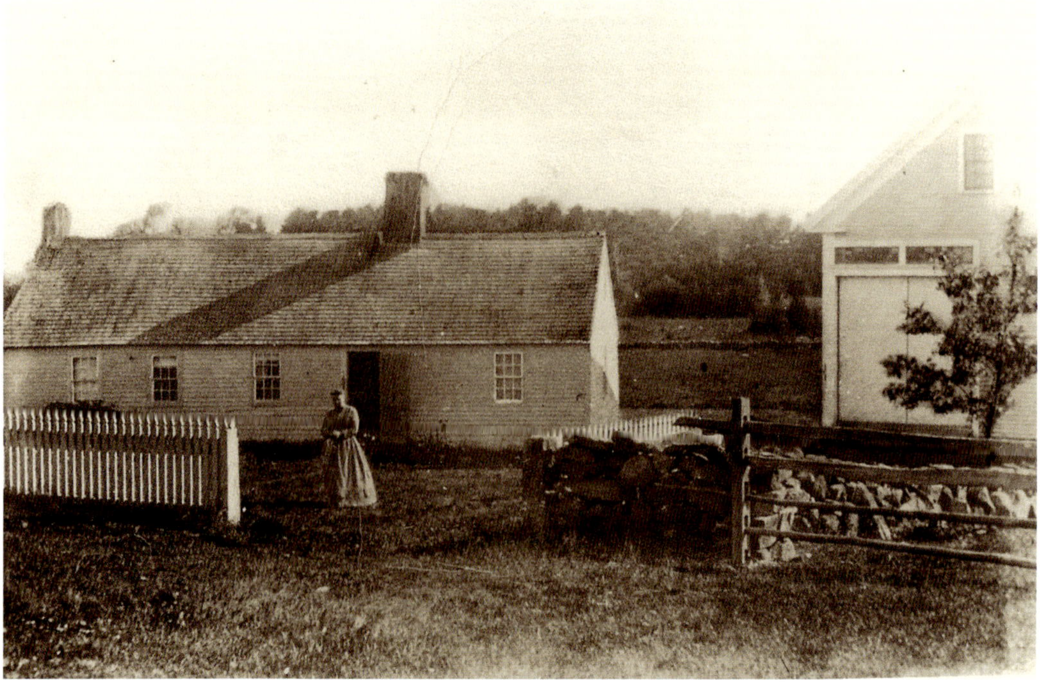

SHOALERS ASHORE: It is said that, at the time of the Revolutionary War, many a Shoaler left the township of Gosport and relocated to "America," floating their homes across miles of ocean. The two photographs of this home in Rye, New Hampshire, were taken *ca.* 1880 and 2014. It sports a plaque that reads "Shoals House - Isaac Remick 1750." Located directly off Route 1A, it is little more than a mile from what is considered a very scenic view of the Isles of Shoals. (SIC/DJC)

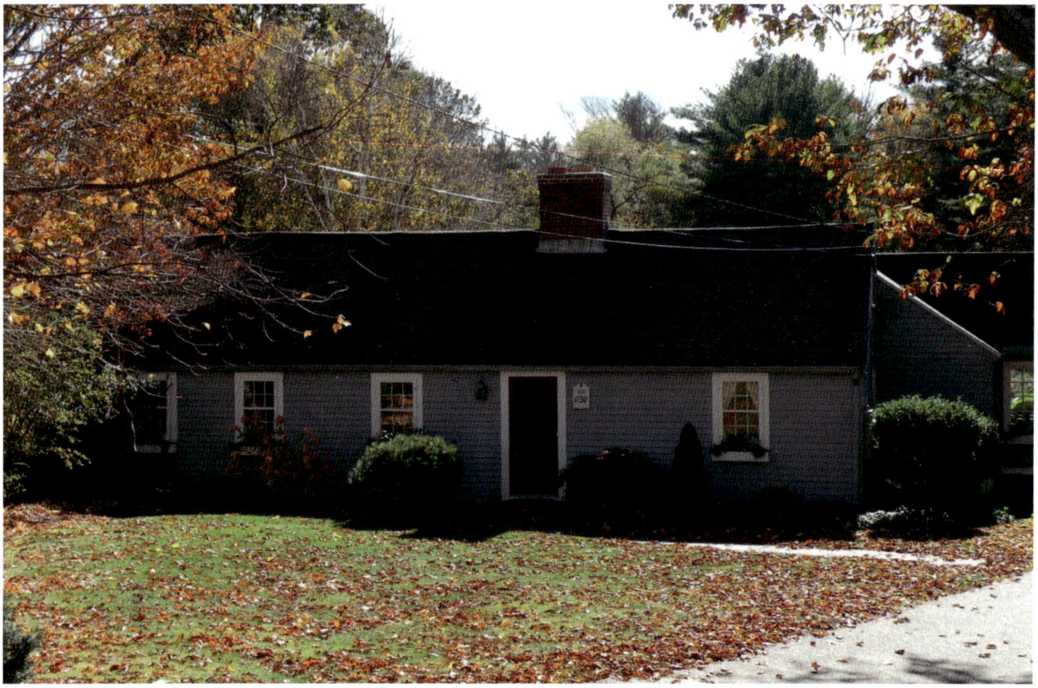

SMUTTYNOSE ISLAND: These two images of Smuttynose Island—*ca.* 1880 and 2018—were taken from nearby Malaga Island. The Haley House is easily identifiable in both photographs, just left of center. To the left of it, the large Mid-Ocean House has been replaced by a smaller house of hospitality, what today's Stewards of Smuttynose Island know as Gull Cottage or, affectionately, Rozzie's. This cottage was built around 1960 by poet and painter Celia Thaxter's granddaughter, Rosamond Thaxter, as a safe haven for stranded seaman. (SIC/DJC)

OLD TURNSTILE: The old turnstile on Star Island is one of countless island "celebrity landmarks." John Smith's monument is clearly seen to the right of the turnstile in the first image, but now barely visible from this similar angle. Notice the shell of a wigwam to the far right in the contemporary image. As part of the 400th anniversary celebration of John Smith's arrival at and mapping of the Isles of Shoals, educators built the wigwam as a way to promote awareness of the history of native American presence on the Isles of Shoals. (SIC/DJC)

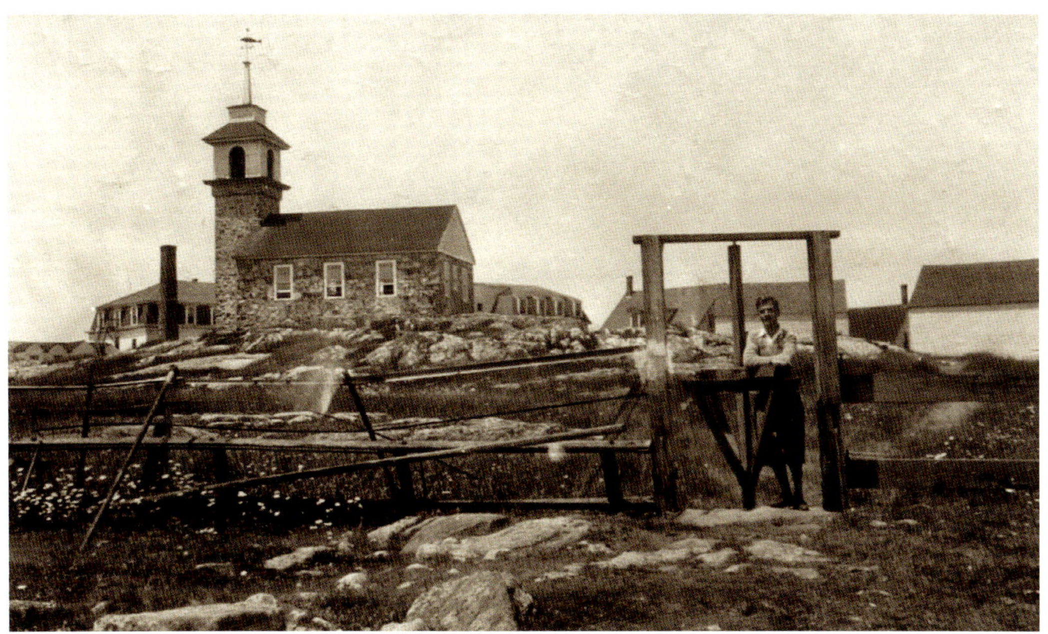

FROM THE OTHER SIDE: Evidently, the turnstile was considered a photo-op even a century ago. Looking north-northwest, a view of what is known as the stone village has replaced that of sections of the Oceanic Hotel and several cottages. Obscuring this view now is (left to right) Vaughn Cottage Museum and Library, Parker, Newton, the Parsonage and Marshman (not seen in this image). A stone wall was reconstructed and replaced the wooden fence, both once used as a dividing line for man and beast. (SIC/DJC)

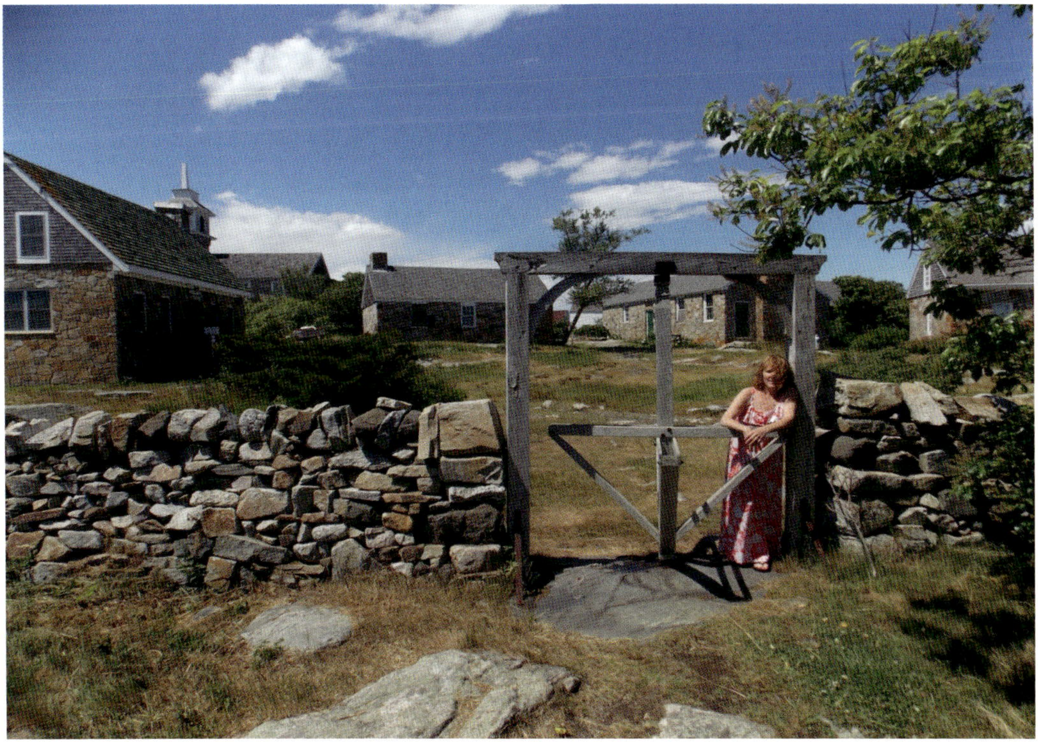

THE BREAKWATER: This breakwater between Star and Cedar islands, built by the U.S. government in 1913-1914, finally created a fully sheltered Gosport Harbor enclosed by Maine's Malaga, Smuttynose, and Cedar Islands, and New Hampshire's Star Island. This couple seen looking towards the east may be contemplating whether pirates really did bury treasure on these isles. (SIC/DJC)

 Featuring the Caswell Cemetery in the foreground and the Oceanic Hotel just behind it, the many similarities in these images speak to Star Island Corporation's and its constituents' commitment to preserve this historic island to the best of their ability. The hotel itself looks almost identical to its earlier self. Having received a five-year grant from the New Hampshire Preservation Society in 2015, Star Island Corporation has undertaken many restoration projects to preserve the hotel including a new roof, siding, windows, structural reinforcement, and more. (SIC/DJC)

 The building seen above, affectionately known as "Shack," has seen many uses over the years, as have many buildings on Star Island. Originally used as a plant to produce gas for the hotel's gaslights, it is now outfitted with an expansive deck and used as staff quarters. In 2018, contractors Kadlik Woodcraft did an extensive interior and exterior renovation on this building. Seen below, to the left of Shack, is now a carpenter shop and a powerhouse. (SIC/DJC)

TENNIS ON STAR: Many a tournament has been played on this tennis court during the past century by conferees, Pelicans and visitors alike. Although some equipment is available at the Oceanic Hotel, it is suggested that the serious tennis player bring his or her own equipment. Note the lack of external fire escapes on the Oceanic and Gosport, now replaced by enclosed fire escapes. Also of note is that the flag once flown atop the hotel has been relocated to the front lawn. Seen below (left to right) are: Cam Duvall, Deb Duvall, Jane Barry, Jessica Cann and Crista Wooley. (SIC/DJC)

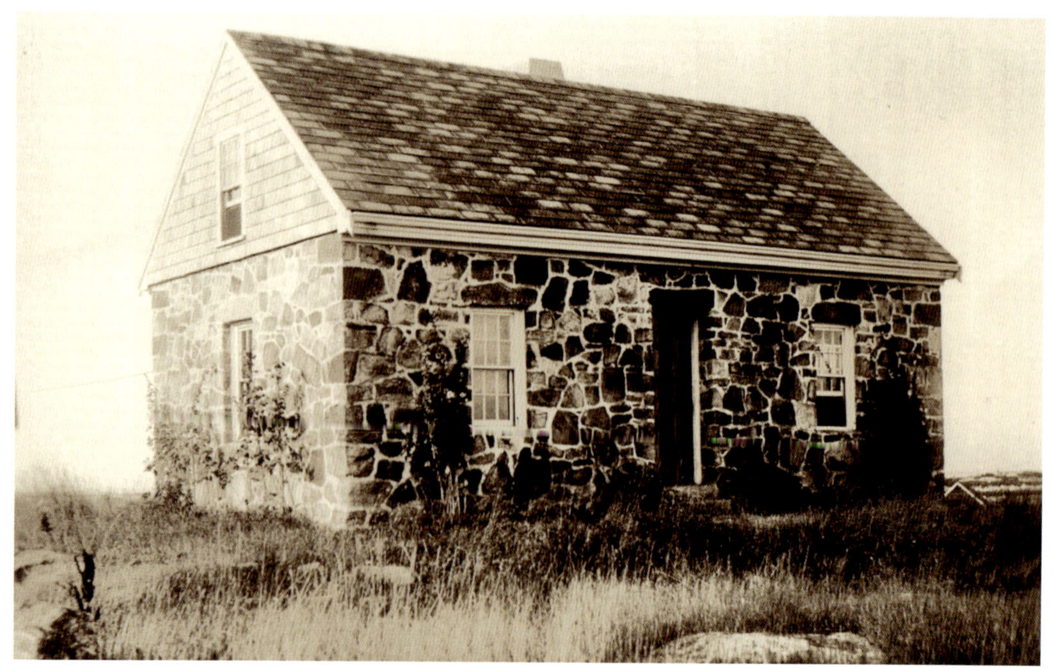

VAUGHN COTTAGE: Built in 1960 from granite cut on Star Island, Vaughn Cottage is the home of the Thaxter Museum and Vaughn Library. It houses a collection that museum professionals have dubbed a "national treasure." Following an in-depth conservation assessment, many of the recommendations were carried out. The old and inadequate vault where many of the museum's most treasured artifacts were housed was replaced with a new vault with year-round climate control built by volunteers. Vaughn consists of an exhibit room and a reading room with a small library of Shoals related books. (SIC/DJC)

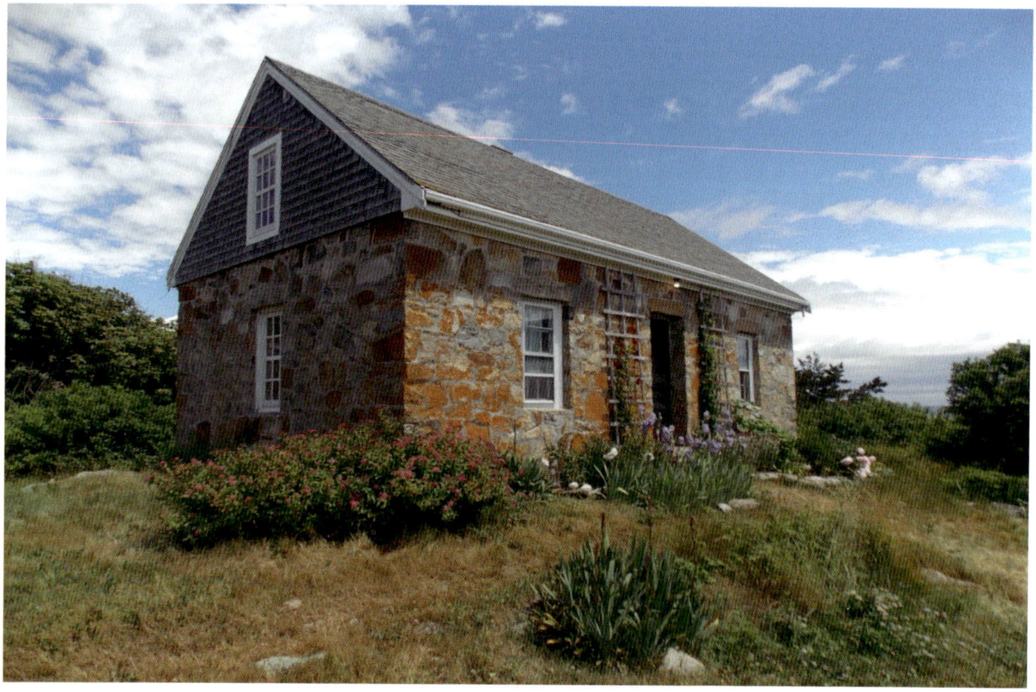

THE LAST RESIDENTS: The large home in the forefront of each photograph—referred to today as Cottage D—was originally built in the mid-1800s by Gosport resident John Bragg Downs. Because Downs and his wife declined to sell their island home to John Poor and lived there until very near the end of their lives, they were the last residents of the town of Gosport. Note the change in location of the chimney on Cottage C (just to the right of Cottage D), and the addition of dormers to Cottage B (directly to the right of Cottage C.) In 2012, dormers were added to Cottage A (not seen in this image). (SIC/DJC)

THE CHAPEL: Star Island's chapel has had many names over the years including the Gosport Meeting House, the Old Stone Church, Gosport Chapel, Gosport Church and Star Island Chapel. It was originally built here on the highest point on the island in the 1680s under the pastorship of Reverend Samuel Belcher. It has since been rebuilt twice on its original site. In these two images one notes the missing weathervane in the contemporary photograph, the wooden tower replaced with stone, and, once again, the lack of vegetation in the early image versus the lush foliage seen today. (SIC/DJC)

TESTAMENT TO CHANGE: The old parsonage, burned in 1904, is visible in the older photograph. The original John Smith Monument is also visible to the right of the chapel. Note a wooden fence stretching out to the right of the chapel and makeshift clotheslines in the foreground. In the contemporary image the gable end of today's stone parsonage, built in 1927 on the original site, is visible to the left of the chapel, as is Newton Center, built in 1952. Newton serves many functions including mess hall for island open-up and close-up staff, social hour gathering place for conferees, lecture hall, art exhibit room and more. Note the access door added to the exterior of the tower. (SIC/DJC)

PROCESSION: The procession of the faithful to the chapel is a beloved tradition on Star Island. As night falls, they gather at the base of the winding path to the chapel, carrying candle lanterns, safely replicating the old whale oil lanterns of yore. It is an image that has been captured by photographers and artists alike. (SIC).

SOLITARY LIGHTS: Once they reach the chapel, the Shoalers hang their lanterns from brackets on the walls of the chapel, and the dancing flames become the solitary sources of light in the building. If anything approximates life on Star in 1900, or even 1800, when the chapel was built, this reenactment does so. (DJC/DJC)

IF THESE WALLS COULD TALK: Many have ministered to the Shoalers from the chapel's pulpit, including Samuel Moody who gave up his ministry to fight the Indians, Josiah Stevens, who served in the Revolutionary War, and, of course, the Reverend John Tucke who was undeniably the most revered by the islanders. Gosport church records reveal numerous entries of spousal breaches of the 7th Commandment: Thou Shalt Not Commit Adultery. The old brick floor, sturdy pews and sensibly designed sconces still reflect a simpler time. (SIC/DJC)

JOHN DOWNS' SKETCHES: Today the old church is still meticulously kept. However, if one sits along the back pews, several old etchings as seen here are visible, some with the initials "JD" carved below them. They may be the sketches of a young John W. Downs. Born in 1870, Downs was the son of native fisherman Ephraim Henry Downs and grew up on the islands. In Downs' memoirs, *Sprays of Salt*, the author includes several sketches of schooners, such as the *Agnes E. Downs*, seen below, which are remarkably similar to those still detectable today, despite many coats of paint. (DJC/*Sprays of Salt*).

JOHN SMITH: The Captain explored the seacoast in 1614, and 250 years later his story still held romance. The Reverend George Beebe conceived of a monument on Star Island to his memory that included depictions of the heads of three Turks Smith claimed to have beheaded during his adventures. Within a few years of its 1864 erection, the original monument began to succumb to the harshness of the local climate. (SIC/SIC)

JOHN SMITH REVIVED: The New Hampshire Society of Colonial Wars refurbished the monument, minus the toppled column, in 1914 in time for the 300th anniversary of his New England explorations, adding a granite pedestal and dedicating a new bronze plaque. Despite a never-ending battle with the elements, the monument continues to stand, now more than 400 years since Smith explored the region to send home news that would attract investors and settlers. (SIC/DJC)

CEDAR ISLAND: Star Island's waterfront is not only utilized for docking boats. Then and now conferees, island staff and visitors have all enjoyed sunbathing on the dock or diving into the chilly waters of the Atlantic Ocean. Cedar Island, seen in the distance, has made headlines more than once. A land dispute involving the Laighton and Caswell families was dubbed "the famous Cedar Island seizure case" by the *Boston Globe* in the 1890s. (SIC)

MURDER: In 1940, the island was again in the news when John Fields, Jr., twenty-two, murdered Stanley Wakem, twenty-one, on a vessel in the middle of Gosport Harbor. As the state line crosses the breakwater between Cedar Island and Star Island, this raised questions regarding which state had jurisdiction—Maine or New Hampshire. Ultimately it was determined that the crime occurred on the Maine side of the harbor. Fields was acquitted of this murder by reason of insanity. He was committed to Augusta State Hospital, from which he escaped—twice! (DJC)

CELIA'S COTTAGE: Visited by artists, musicians and literary beacons of the late nineteenth century, Celia Thaxter's cottage was unfortunately taken by the Appledore Hotel fire in 1914. Her parlor, filled with artistry, and her prolific, colorful island garden inspired many. The cottage to the right of Celia's cottage, also taken by the same fire, was known as the Richter cottage. Today, Celia's revered and colorful garden has been recreated for Appledore Island visitors to enjoy. In addition to her garden, a raised deck representing her lovely porch, or piazza, overlooking the garden has also been rebuilt. (SIC/DJC)

LAIGHTON CEMETERY: In a clearing near the top of a small hill on Appledore Island is the Laighton family cemetery. All five members of the immediate Laighton family chose to be laid to rest on this island where they spent the majority of their lives. It is a testament to their love of each other and the place they called home that Thomas and Eliza's three adult children—Celia, Oscar and Cedric—chose to lie here together for eternity even though two of the three had spouses and children on the mainland. According to Mrs. Frederick Delano, Celia's cousin, Thomas Laighton, insisted on being buried with his back to the mainland. (SIC/DJC)

CELIA'S VIEW: These two photographs were taken from almost the exact same location overlooking Celia Thaxter's gardens, the original and the recreation. The bathing pool is now completely obstructed by vegetation. At least three buildings which withstood the fire of 1914 are visible in the center of both photographs: Laighton House, Hamilton, and the old Life-Saving Service station built in 1910 by the U.S. government. (SIC)

ONCE AND ALWAYS HOME: Laighton House now houses three small lecture halls and a small library and study area. Hamilton is now utilized as administrative headquarters on the second floor, and a larger lecture hall on the first floor. The Coast Guard Station is now known as Bartels and serves as staff residence. A bird banding station is located in the central valley where the hotel once stood. To the far right is a World War II radar tower which is utilized for storage. (DJC)

Beebe Cemetery: Located in a hollow at the south end of Star Island stands a memorial to Reverend George Beebe, minister to the island from 1856 through 1869, and the graves of his three young daughters who tragically died within days of each other from illness. A map drawn in 1854 lists this area as a cemetery ten years before little sisters Mittie, Millie and Jessie died, suggesting this was a "repurposed" burial ground. (SIC/DJC)

DUDLEY MOORE: At the south end of Star Island, tucked beneath a rock ledge located just above Beebe Cemetery is a square stone plaque engraved "Dudley Moore 1901 – 1937." This remote location chosen to memorialize Moore captivates adventurers today. In 1939, two years after Moore's death, a Mrs. Dudley Moore of Montreal, Canada—quite probably Moore's widow—directed a stunt program and costume party in Elliott Hall as part of the Religious Education Institute Conference at Star Island on Thursday, July 20th. (SIC/DJC)

BABB'S COVE: Philip Babb was an early settler and constable at the Shoals and left a substantial estate upon his death in 1671. In the 1600s, Babb's Cove on Appledore Island was bustling with fishing vessels in the 1600s. During the Laighton era, Babb's Cove, known then as the "bathing pool," was popular with guests of the Appledore Hotel as a saltwater swimming pool complete with bathhouses, a safe rowing area and place for young guests to engage in boat races. (SIC/DJC)

A COTTAGE FOR ABBIE: Built on the southern end of Appledore Island by Oscar Laighton for his cousin Abbie in 1910, this house has changed little through time. Thanks to its location, it survived the fire that took the Appledore Hotel and many of its other cottages in 1914. Today, Stewards on neighboring Smuttynose Island report enjoying sitting on the front lawn in front of Haley House watching the revolving light from White Island Lighthouse shine on this cottage in the evenings. (SIC/DJC)

THE LIFE-SAVING STATION: Built to withstand the worst that Mother Nature can throw at it, the Isles of Shoals Life-Saving Station grew out of an age of "wooden ships and iron men," when "surfmen" jumped into small boats to row into the teeth of gales to save mariners in distress at sea. Though built late in the Life-Saving Service period, in 1910, the station remained active into the Coast Guard years, post 1915, and today is part of the Shoals Marine Lab complex. (SIC/DJC)

THE COAST GUARD BOATHOUSE: Marine railways led from the doors of the boathouse to the waters below, helping the Coast Guardsmen on Appledore Island launch their lifeboats and surfboats on the way to rescues. To return, they needed the assistance of a powered winch. Over time, the surfmen left the station, the station fell to the ground and the only thing that remains is the engine that pulled that winch, an unlikely monument to a bygone era. (SIC/DJC)

SURFMEN REMEMBERED: The Keepers and Surfmen of the Isles of Shoals Life-Saving Station toiled through day and night, coastal storms and long periods of boredom. The Coast Guardsmen who followed them protected local boaters kept a presence until the end of World War II. Today they are remembered by a memorial bench, an appropriate thank you for men—and at that time, they were all men—who stood *Semper Paratus*, or "Always Ready" to help. (SIC/DJC)

Radar Station: At seven stories tall, the concrete Base End or Radar Station is conspicuous to say the least, and mysterious at the same time. Built in 1944, the station supported nearby Forts Dearborn and Foster through targeting for numerous local coastal artillery batteries, anti-aircraft intelligence and, during the war, a steel frame radar unit that once stood 50 feet above the concrete. Like all island structures, it has faced serious deterioration due to the elements (SIC/DJC).

A SURPRISE FOR LYMAN RUTLEDGE: Planning and funding of the original Brookfield Youth Center and Rutledge Marine Laboratory was apparently quite a secret project. Not even namesake Lyman Rutledge was aware of it. Dubbed "The Six Conspirators" by Rutledge, a group of women conceived the idea and sought the funding to build and equip it. Donald and Phyllis Brookfield were instrumental in its building and donated funds in memory of their son, Lt. Douglas H. Brookfield, USAF. Contractor Dominic Gratta was hired. Gratta had been a key figure in the building of Appledore Island's marine biology lab for the education of Cornell University students. Construction of the Brookfield-Rutledge Marine Lab began in August 1970.

The roof was kept low to retain an unfettered view of Gosport Harbor. When it came time to lift its 40-foot-long 1,200-pound beams, good ol' Star Island ingenuity was needed. Using an old 1952 Chevy pickup truck, a makeshift winch, staging and a chainfall, Gratta and his crew got the job done!

The building officially opened in 1971. Its cement floor was built to support heavy sea tables, which were filled each season with lobster, hermit crabs, sea stars, urchins and more often collected by local fishmen, lobstermen and divers from Cornell at Appledore. There was also a large tank that was constructed using the granite bedrock from Star Island.

A New Brookfield-Rutledge: In 2019 a new Brookfield-Rutledge Marine Lab was erected on the site of the original building. It was built to withstand rogue waves, flooding due to storm surges, and even earthquakes! Director of Facilities, Jack Farrell, conveys it is 20 inches higher than the original building—lifting it out of the dirt to avoid rot. Its extensive concrete footing system is rooted in bedrock. Galvanized I-beam supports and a heavily built floor system allows for a large assembly space while meeting current occupancy codes. The marine lab has been enlarged and its water supply and electrical systems upgraded. The large fish tank originally constructed of Star Island granite remains. Bathrooms have been enlarged and made more accessible. And, importantly, the building is now on the island fire system.

The Rutledge Marine Lab sports educational panels that illustrate Star Island's history including early indigenous peoples, marine environment, the Green Gosport Initiative effort and more.

VIEWS OF LUNGING ISLAND: Evident by the windmill in the early twentieth-century image above is Star Island Corporation's commitment to green energy even then. Today, the island is nearly self-sufficient. The Summer House to the right in each photograph has been rebuilt, but still stands on the site of the original stone Fort Star. Low-lying, privately owned Lunging Island, once owned by Oscar Laighton, is also visible in each image. (SIC/DJC)

HONEYMOON COTTAGE: The cottage looks quite the same as when Oscar Laighton built it on Lunging Island in the late nineteenth century. Reverend Frank Ferguson bought the island in the 1920s. His grandson, Malcom Ferguson, was a close friend, confidant and advisor to Reverend Lyman Rutledge, one of Star Island's patriarchs throughout much of the twentieth century. Lunging Island is now owned by the Randall family and a beautiful guest cottage has been added. (SIC/DJC)

ENGINEER'S: These two images of what is known as Engineer's Cottage were captured fifty years apart. Engineer's is one of the older buildings on Star Island and presumably was once a fisherman's home during the Gosport era. Shack, dormitory-style housing for island workers can be seen peeking out from behind the cottage. The view of White and Seavey Islands is now obscured by the island's Carpenter Shop. The flat-roofed building to its right is the Powerhouse for the island. The power lines in the older photograph have since been buried underground. Also, a small porch has been added to Engineer's. (SIC/DJC)

REGATTAS: In the nineteenth century, when yachting was young, regattas were tourist attractions that beckoned people to the coast. The allure remains today. Whether part of an official race or simply the backdrop to a gorgeous summer day on the ocean, a billowed sail can speak of nothing but pleasures spent by the seaside. (SIC/DJC)

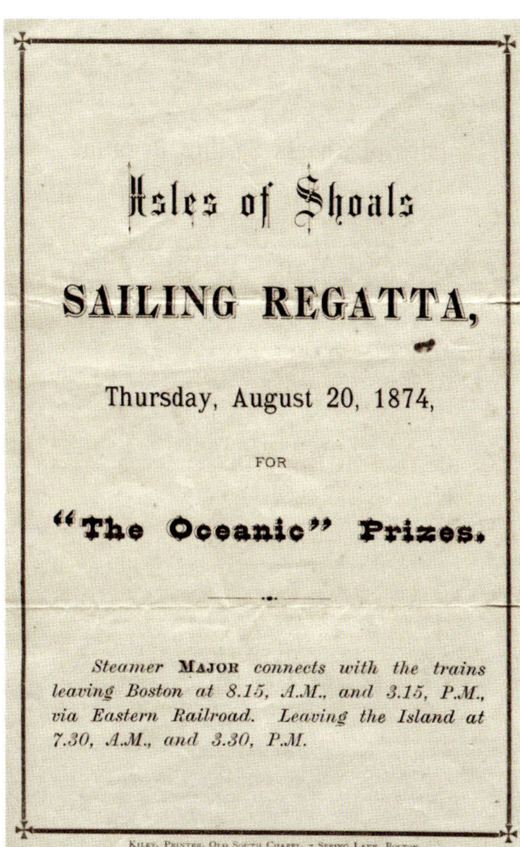

Isles of Shoals

SAILING REGATTA,

Thursday, August 20, 1874,

FOR

"The Oceanic" Prizes.

Steamer **MAJOR** *connects with the trains leaving Boston at 8.15, A.M., and 3.15, P.M., via Eastern Railroad. Leaving the Island at 7.30, A.M., and 3.30, P.M.*

KILEY, PRINTER, OLD SOUTH CHAPEL, 7 SPRING LANE, BOSTON.

A Distant Light: These two images look towards White and Seavey Islands from the southwest side of Star Island. White Island Lighthouse, sometimes referred to as the Isles of Shoals Light, was built in 1821. It originally sported a red, white and blue light. Coincidentally, both images capture a vessel passing behind the two islands and at a similar tide. The Victorian-style keeper's house seen in the older image was built in 1877. This house was replaced with the simpler Cape-style house in the early 1950s. White Island Light is now owned by New Hampshire State Parks. (SIC/DJC)

WHITE ISLAND LIGHTHOUSE: White Island Light itself has been through many changes through the years, from a simple lantern in the window of an island resident, to a new lighthouse built in 1821 and a new one built after that in 1859. In 1986, the Coast Guard left the island as the light was automated. The covered walkway was washed away in 2007 and rebuilt with a federal grant to the state of New Hampshire in 2011. It remains today, a blessing to anyone making the trip from house to tower during a coastal storm. (SIC/DJC).

ROCKS: Until one stands
on the edge of the sea, until
one witnesses the power of
the ocean and the stubborn
nature of the rock on which
the Isles of Shoals are built,
there can be no way to fully
explain the sensations one
gets. Inspiration may be an
appropriate word, as the proof
is in the canvases, the poetry,
prose and music that has been
composed by Shoals visitors.

RETURNS: Through the ages people have come back to the Isles of Shoals. For few has it been a one-and-done vacation spot. Every visitor has a favored hangout, a quiet place for reflection, a place that is first on the agenda upon arrival. For some, it is where romance begins, in the form of notes in bottles tossed into the sea, to make distant connections with fellow beachcombers and ocean gazers. (SIC/DJC)

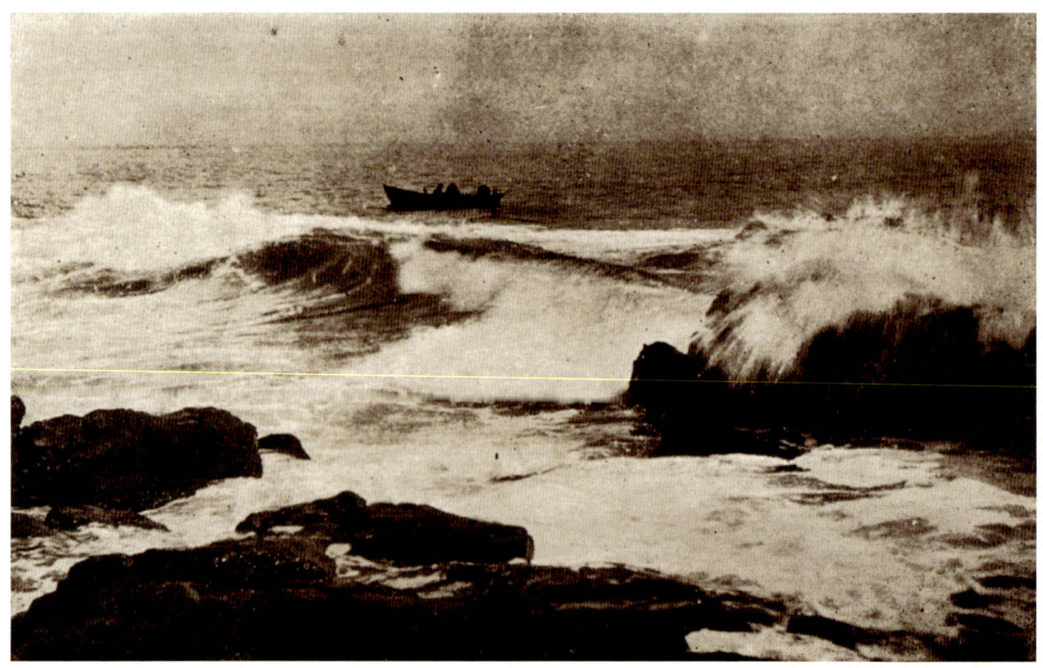

OFFSHORE: While gazing out onto that sea, one might get a true sense of the history of the Isles of Shoals, for it was the fishermen who built it so many decades ago. Without the power of motors, driven only by winds, tides and currents, they braved the bashing of the waves upon the shore and created a town, a culture and an economy all their own. Ghostlike, similar scenes reappear today. (SIC/DJC)

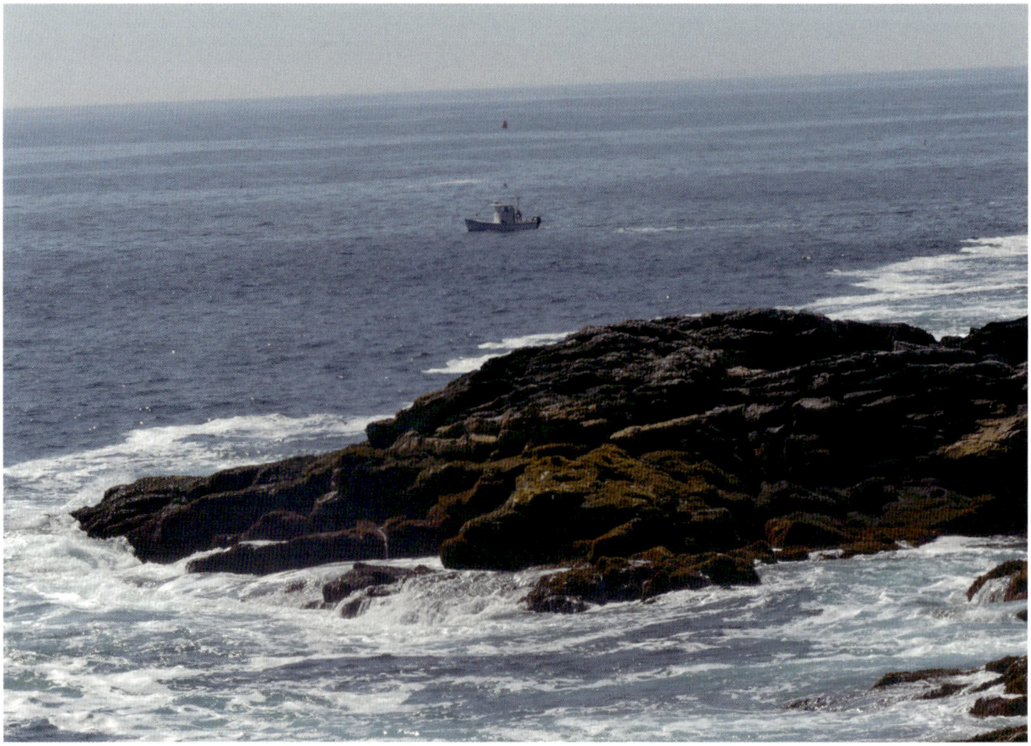

3

Getting There is Half the Fun

A boat ride is inevitable if one wants to reach the Shoals. For more than a century and a half, boat operators have safely carried passengers from the mainland to the islands aboard an array of vessels that, despite the passage of time, have not evolved to look very differently than they did when the first seasonal visitors arrived in the post-Civil War years. Here we explore the various boats that have brought us to, from and around the Isles of Shoals (DJC).

OCEANIC AND VIKING SUN: The earliest steamboats to serve the Shoals were the *Pioneer* (1866-1868) and the *Appledore* (1869-1885). In 1873, the Oceanic Hotel had a steamboat called *Major*. In 1875 the *Appledore* served both islands. The *Major*, after a fire, was rebuilt and called the *Oceanic* (1886-1900). This is the *Oceanic* at Star Island pier. The Viking Cruise Company ran two boats to Star Island from 1980 to 1987. They were the *Viking Queen* and the *Viking Sun*. Below is the *Viking Sun*. (PA/SIC)

CITY OF PORTSMOUTH AND THOMAS LAIGHTON: The *City of Portsmouth* took passengers from Boston to Portsmouth and the Shoals in the 1880s. The ship is also listed as working Martha's Vineyard in the 1880s. In 1892, the steamer provided service from Beverly, Salem Willows, Marblehead and Boston, Massachusetts, and was lost after striking Aqua Vitae Ledge near Salem the same year. The *Thomas Laighton*, designed to look like a nineteenth-century steamboat, ran between 1987-2004 and 2010 to present. (PA/DJC)

CAPTAIN'S LADY AND THOMAS LAIGHTON: Between 2005 and 2009, Star Island Corporation contracted with Captain's Fishing Parties of Newburyport, Massachusetts, to service Star Island. The photo above shows the *Captain's Lady* and the *Captain's Lady II* at Rye Harbor, New Hampshire, where the service originated. The boats had a capacity of 150 passengers each and for large conferences both boats were needed. The *Thomas Laighton* came back in 2010. In 2013 Captains Jerod Blanchette and Jeremy Bell purchased the Isles of Shoals Steamship Company (ISSCO) from Robin Whittaker. (DJC/DJC)

PINAFORE AND SAKONNET: The *Pinafore*, named for the Gilbert and Sullivan comic opera *HMS Pinafore*, was a small boat that made trips among the islands and was the winter link to the mainland. She was the launch that carried staff, guests and freight. She is the subject of Childe Hassam's painting "Moonlight, 1890." Dave Reynolds, a former facilities manager on Star, contracted the *Sakonnet*, originally designed to be a sailboat, to transport freight and staff between 2007 and 2008. (SIC/SIC)

PAMELA J. THAYER II AND MISS JULIE: The original *Pamela J* (1994-2000) formerly known as the *Pauline*, was a gift from Rev. Bob J. Thayer in memory of his wife. The boat in the photo is the *Pamela J. Thayer II*. She is a 38' "Novi" style commercial boat formally named *Desiree's Dream*. She worked between 2002 and 2010. The *Miss Julie* is a 29' lobster boat built by Wayne Beal of Jonesport, Maine. She was contracted from Jack Farrell, a Star Island facilities manager. (SIC/DJC)

KINGSBURY AND HURRICANE: Here, the *John M. Kingsbury* is on the way to Appledore in 1990. She was built in 1984 for the Shoals Marine Laboratory. The *Hurricane* is a wooden boat built in Southwest Harbor, Mount Desert Island, Maine, in 1967 for the Hurricane Island Outward Bound School. In 1996-1997 she worked in Boston for Thompson Island and University of Massachusetts, 1996-2006. In 2006 she was sold to Downeast Sailing Adventures in Bar Harbor, Maine. Jack Farrell acquired her in 2017. (RT/DJC)

SAM ADAMS AND UTOPIA:
The *Pinafore* sank in the Portland Gale of 1898. She was replaced by the motor launch *Sam Adams*. She is noted for her participation in the rescue attempt of Star Island waitresses who sadly drowned in 1902. Royal Lowell designed the *Utopia*, 42 feet long and able to carry twenty, which was built in Newington, New Hampshire, in 1974. She worked as fishing boat hunting Atlantic Bluefin Tuna. Jack Farrell acquired her in 2015 and contracted with Star to provide sunset, lobster, and sightseeing cruises for Star's guests. (SIC/DJC)

VIKING STAR AND CHALLENGER: The *Viking Star* (1968-1975) worked in the time between the *Viking Queen* and the *Viking Sun*. The *Challenger*, which has similar lines to the *Viking Star*, was added to the ISSCO in 2016. She was launched in Newburyport, Massachusetts, at the Hilton Yard as a fishing party boat in 1970. Her hull is mahogany. She is 60 feet long and carries ninety-eight passengers. Her original name was *Capt. Red*. (SIC/DJC)

UNCLE OSCAR AND UNCLE OSCAR: Sue Reynolds started a boat business in 1992 at Rye Harbor, New Hampshire. She bought the 38-foot, 21-passenger boat *Blackback* out of York, Maine, and changed its name to *Uncle Oscar*. It made daily trips to Star Island. In 2017 Sue retired and sold the boat to an owner in Martha's Vineyard. Sue's son Pete continued the business with a 62-foot, forty-nine-passenger boat, a former fishing charter from Arundel, Maine. (DJC/DJC)

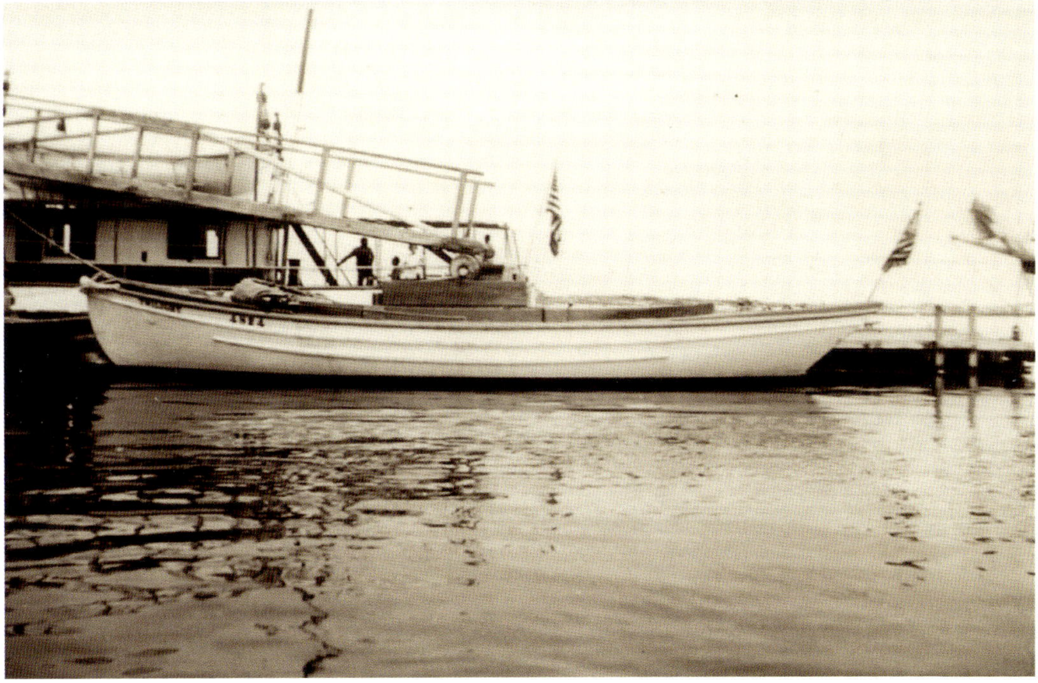

TWILIGHT AND DUDLEY: Oscar Laighton, in his later years, owned a launch with a gasoline engine called the *Twilight*. He gave tours around the islands to guests and staff, and also used it for personal purposes. In 2015 the launch *Dudley* came to Star Island. The *Dudley* is employed in carrying boaters, guests and staff to boats in the harbor and other islands. (SIC/DJC)

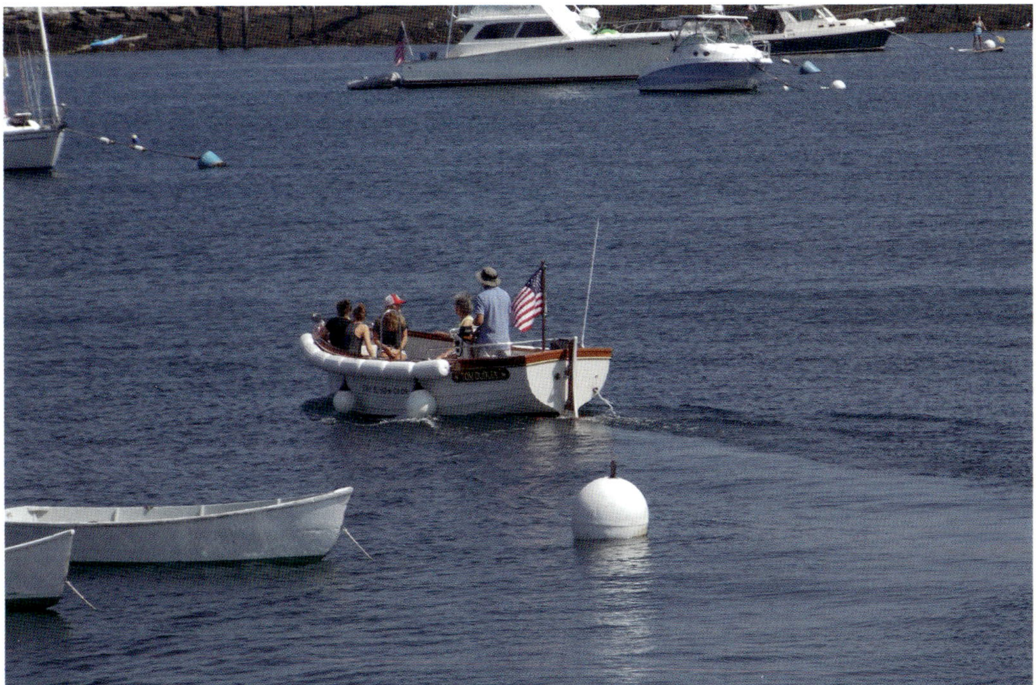

PELICAN AND ALMOST BLUE: In the 1920s, a staff member owned a sailboat called the *Pelican*. The staff members who sailed the boat were called the Pelicans. Eventually all the young staffers working on Star became known as Pelicans. The *Almost Blue*, owned by the Pelican Club, when restored, will sail again. The boat is a Cape Dory Typhoon Weekender designed by Carl Arlberge, built in East Taunton, Massachusetts, between 1967 and 1985 as hull number two. Adam Shapiro, in the photo, helped with the restoration. (SIC/DJC)

ROWING JUST FOR FUN: Two ladies are rowing in the Bathing Pool at Appledore Island. They are not going anywhere, getting wet, or getting too much sun. The two women today are coming back to Star Island from having a swim at Smuttynose Island. (SIC/DJC)

GOSPORT REGATTA: John Poor organized the Gosport Regatta (1874-1875) to promote the Oceanic Hotel. The yacht *America* raced in both regattas. The course started at Gosport Harbor around Boon Island and back to Gosport Harbor. In 2010, the first modern Regatta was organized by the Piscataqua Sailing Association in cooperation with Star Island Corporation. This race begins at Portsmouth, buoy 2KR, rounds White Island and ends at Gosport Harbor. The old photo shows boats in Gosport Harbor. The 2018 photo shows boats rounding White Island. (SIC/DJC)

ARRIVALS AND DEPARTURES: Greeting boats arriving at Star is done with a smile and a wave. Boats leaving Star are sent with a traditional chant, "S-T-A-R, S-T-A-R, Oceanic, Oceanic, Rah, Rah, Rah, you will come back, you will come back," is shouted from the pier. The response from the boats is, "We will come back, we will come back." The boat is the *Viking* (1962-1968). (SIC/SIC)

A Cheer and a Wave: Here, the *Thomas Laighton* is greeted on arrival on one of the last days of the season. Note she leans to the left as the passengers line up to get off. The launch with the letters "PYC" is from the Portsmouth Yacht Club coming to help with the 2018 Regatta. Three Pelicans are sending friends off in the *Miss Julie* with a cheer and a wave. (DJC/DJC)

GOING HOME: This is the *Sightseer*, which in 1941 was the last steamboat to serve the Isles of Shoals. It is most likely on its last trip of the day to Portsmouth. The second photo is one of the last sailboats from the 2018 Regatta on its trip home, sailing into the sunset. (SIC/DJC)

ACKNOWLEDGMENTS

The authors wish to thank the Star Island office staff, including Joe Watts, who encouraged us to produce this book; Kate Brady, who answered many questions; and Ally Miner, for many important bits of support. We'd like to thank the staff of the Portsmouth Athenaeum their assistance; Adam Shapiro, who provided background on the Pelican Club *Almost Blue* sailboat restoration; Tim O'Connor, of the Isles of Shoals Steamship Company; Dave Reynolds, for information on his boat *Sakonnet*; Jack Farrell for information on his boats *Miss Julie, Hurricane,* and *Utopia*; Peter Reynolds, for information on *Uncle Oscar*; Mark Nash, for rides to the islands to take the modern photos; Gretchen Gudeain for the Isles of Shoals Historical Research Association postcard; Devin Kish, Vaughn Cottage curator, 2018; Bruce Parsons and Tom Mansfield, who were always available to answer questions; Star Island's Roger Trudeau for boating us around the islands; Appledore Island Coordinator Collin Love; Appledore Island Assistant Coordinator Taylor Oullette; and every person who wilfully posed for a photo for this book. Our heartfelt thanks go to our families, for their support, both spiritual and editorial, especially in the case of Janet, Jessica and Emily Cann. Images came courtesy of Star Island Corporation (SIC); Donald J. Cann (DJC); Courtesy of the Portsmouth Athenaeum (PA); Library of Congress (LOC); Isles of Shoals Historical Research Association (ISHRA); Ron Titus (RT); (PHS) Portsmouth Historical Society Collection, photos courtesy of the Portsmouth Athenaeum; (*Sprays of Salt*) *Sprays of Salt: Reminiscences of a Native Shoaler*.